A Brilliant Loss

A Brilliant Loss

POEMS

Eloise Klein Healy

Red Hen Press | *Pasadena, CA*

Book Design by Mark E. Cull

Library of Congress Cataloging-in-Publication Data

Names: Healy, Eloise Klein, author.
Title: A brilliant loss: poems / Eloise Klein Healy.
Description: First edition. | Pasadena, CA: Red Hen Press, [2022]
Identifiers: LCCN 2022007377 (print) | LCCN 2022007378 (ebook) | ISBN
    9781636280615 (paperback) | ISBN 9781636280622 (ebook)
Subjects: LCGFT: Poetry.
Classification: LCC PS3558.E234 B75 2022 (print) | LCC PS3558.E234
    (ebook) | DDC 811/.54—dc23/eng/20220224
LC record available at https://lccn.loc.gov/2022007377
LC ebook record available at https://lccn.loc.gov/2022007378

The National Endowment for the Arts, the Los Angeles County Arts Commission, the Ahmanson Foundation, the Dwight Stuart Youth Fund, the Max Factor Family Foundation, the Pasadena Tournament of Roses Foundation, the Pasadena Arts & Culture Commission and the City of Pasadena Cultural Affairs Division, the City of Los Angeles Department of Cultural Affairs, the Audrey & Sydney Irmas Charitable Foundation, the Meta & George Rosenberg Foundation, the Albert and Elaine Borchard Foundation, the Adams Family Foundation, Amazon Literary Partnership, the Sam Francis Foundation, and the Mara W. Breech Foundation partially support Red Hen Press.

First Edition
Published by Red Hen Press
www.redhen.org

ACKNOWLEDGMENTS

The author wishes to thank the following publications in which some of these poems first appeared:

Alaska Quarterly Review: "Aphasia's Not What I Can't Say," "Monday," "Sustain me"; *Bear Review*: "Level 3, Northridge Rehab," "Patient"; *Evocations*: "Just In Case"; *Lavender Review*: "Daring, Darling," "Palm Springs"; *MacGuffin* 38, no. 1: "Flurry of Speaking," "Pleasantry," "The Day Torn"; *Notre Dame Review*: "My Life Before"; *Pacifica Literary Review*: "Down," "Gone," "How Aphasia Zipped Me Up"; *Pangyrus*: "Once, More Than Once," "Slurring"; *Passengers Journal*: "If You Knew"; *Pigeon Pages*: "APHASIA," "My Brain Sizzled, April 2013"; *SLANT*: "Zipped Me Up"; *The Dewdrop*: "Iris"; *Worcester Review*: "My Lazy Eye"; *Words & Whispers*: "Releasing the Tears Again"; and *ZiN Daily*: "The First Effort," "What's the Whole Thing?"

CONTENTS

A Brilliant Loss

Aphasia is an impairment of language, affecting the production or comprehension of speech and the ability to read or write.

—National Aphasia Association

... you say there are not words to describe it, you say it does not exist. But remember. Make an effort to remember. Or, failing that, invent.

—Monique Wittig, *Les Guerilleres* 1971

RELEASING THE TEARS AGAIN

Here's the worst thing I've learned.
My brain ripped alongside my *aphasia*
and, thereafter, nothing "remembered" my language.

I have a different brain now,
but all told, I'm just "new" again,
close to what I write and read.
What I see is clearing the path
to my workroom door.

Emptiness of the space dissolves
as I open it, but that room lifts me,
knowing again for more years
than I could count.

When I was thirty-seven
and bigger than my blessing,
I fell on my knees
spilling moonlight through the window.

I fell on my knees and promised
that poetry would be everything,
the basis of all choices, and here it is again.

THE FIRST EFFORT

I want a thousand drop-dead poems
and no fear to finish more of them.

My art has promised fruition
to have re-written so well.

This passion, like instinct,
is an animal way for the sinew

to wrap my finger on the arrow
and a flight that never, never misses.

MY BRAIN SIZZLED, APRIL 2013

Because of the loss of my language,
I was saying something kind of "brain-messed."
But Colleen kept talking to me,
me not knowing what I said even when I said it.

My own "missing ideas." Nothing mattered anymore.
Nothing spoke to me *about* me,
about my sweetheart, Colleen.

I was certainly missing, but alive anyway.
How can I describe that right there?

WHAT'S THE WHOLE THING?

I cry sometimes
because I remember
I had lost my name,
I mean, my words.

Also, regained the poems
I had written
and books I had loved.

What I said before,
I can't always remember
my former self.

It's not me about fame or money.
Enjoyment is what actually
costs me nothing.

My poems maintain
my writing each day.
Doing it all again.

A P H A S I A

Another day, another duller?
Please tell me or I'll tell you
How the dates and times are feelings
About me. How I lost it
So quickly my language
Itself lost me and I couldn't
Assist myself. Lost it. Found it later.

APHASIA'S NOT WHAT I CAN'T SAY

I know where I am
but can't call it a table.
I also don't know how to say lamp
or couch, chair, armoire, bathroom.
Dishwasher, no.

I first practice what's missing
in the kitchen or living room.
I've had to practice with my sink,
5:00 a.m. teapot, and dining room table
near the microwave.
Haven't practiced the den, office,
bedroom and the stars above.

My list needs help.
Colleen repeats it,
links my words,
linking the ones used
before I lost it all.

BLUEBERRY

All the changes of words,
I wait again today.

My mind needs time
with names and the missing energy.

Please remember—
what I have hoped for.

A clear dragon.
The luminous day.

I am changing my mind.
I can heal.

DOWN

Using my right hand, I point,
"I can draw it."
I drew "Eloise," but really,
it was the opposite angle.

As happy as I am showing
my word backwards,
my point doesn't work.
Missing again.

FIRST I WROTE ABOUT APHASIA

Now I'm adding coronavirus
since this is fuckin' scary.
So, I say then, get in gear, bend and stretch.
Take a deep breath.

Coronavirus is what it knows
just about itself,
a red eye snatching and attaching,
weaving and cranking with whispers.

I think I might even die now, too,
but just for the heck of it
it's easy for me to think about me.

"Say no words," the virus says.
The silent weave, the virus spends
grabbing right next to anybody.

Yet I mean no death to me.
I mean surviving
and that's what I want

All I can be.

GONE

I lost my language so quickly
no real words could even assist me.
I couldn't speak my meanings,
my mouth without my mind
it was just yesterday when I was seventy-two.

HOW APHASIA ZIPPED ME UP

My damaged brain blocked
me in a list and that unsaved me.

I didn't hear what Colleen meant,
I couldn't say what I said to her

and that even lost me
because it lost me first.

HOW TO PLAN

Here's how to plan to
"get my shit together."
I'm flying to Arizona. Just flying
alone now, but not because
I have four or five poetry events
to meet "on the road again."

It's common to lose
what I knew before
brain waves left me behind.

A new world in view, right?
Reminds me of John Keats
staring into how life and death meet.
Now I've learned *to* learn aphasia.
Knocked on my door, then
a new kind of opening.

MAYBE IF A NAME MATTERED

What would the stacks of this email
mean now in my home?
First, aphasia really mattered to me
since I'd lost everything.
My names, my pages, my poetry.

My life has re-mattered my *own* aphasia,
taught me my heart's pure attempts
to lean into myself, to re-live, to re-learn.

Tough writing poems for many years,
it still means that everything I do
means re-writing, then re-working my poetry again.

TURNING LIKE A FIGURE SKATER

Ok, I think I'd been learning to walk
so how did I figure it out?

The doctor listened while I talked,
but me pausing and turning like a figure skater.

Someday I will be able
to re-name myself just fine.

Just laureate, poetry and art.

MY LIFE BEFORE

A slender aphasia altered my brain,
bound and zipped, my shape was not my skill.
I was the haywire that fuzzed my normality
and me empty as a doubt.

So, my goal led me trying to talk,
practicing walks, sleeping during the night.
I ate all my food but I hardly complained,
sometimes I just asked my name again.

It is a big deal now because I was just *missing* words.
Even trying to breathe deeply,
writing and re-editing again.
Loving my words again.
My language. My friend.

PATIENT

At 8:00 a.m., the doctor asked,
"Do you feel pain? How are you walking?"
I know he is speaking *to* me,
but I'm not even able
to remember my name.

LEVEL 3, NORTHRIDGE REHAB

I don't know words well enough
but it's pretty busy to hear it,
then read, spelling one at a time.

No matter, I'm being helped
while I'm walking,
my balance isn't teasing
or touching me, just laughing a little.

My waist is handled and guided
to where my own room has a window.
Don't know everything
about where I lived before.

NOT AGAIN

I hadn't been able to spell
or even remember my name.

Everything unbalanced or out of touch,
something not even a language.

What about remembering
how to eat, walk, still even mumble?

My difficult life was aiming at a beginning.
Certainly most painful, but not yet anything *again*.

NO MUSIC ON THE WARD

The nurses walking with me
and we're swaying, then me lying down.
No music now, women not singing,
nothing adding me up.

Room to room each night
Coughing and moaning,
some ladies cry slowly,
not adding anyone on our list.

Slowly missing me a bit.
Missing.

ONCE, MORE THAN ONCE

Huffing and puffing, Dr. Frye arrived
late in the evening to visit Northridge Hospital.

Frey would worry about my tragedy, already learning
my brain had dropped it, lost.

My ability to speak properly, gone.
It was my aphasia in "outer space."

How could I know anything anymore?
How would I know what to say?

Repeat, how would I know what to say?

PLEASANTRY

My helpers could swing and sway
and lead me to my bed.
When I tried to laugh,
it wasn't quite the problem.

I had to talk and talk and walk
but I could be *so* funny.
My "hello"s seemed meaningful,
saying something normal.
But when I think my body-parts
were good, some were just missing.

Wearing my little "out" jacket
but smart as a brain, my helper wrote
my name HEALY on my L.L. Bean tag.

Who put it there?
Who lost me?

SLURRING

Colleen kept asking me a question
and when I answered, words were slipping,
me slurring my language.

Maybe I was tired, blurring my words.
My mumbling meant
some of me was missing.

So, here my words answered,
but not thinking *aphasia* meant "missing."
I didn't know it then, knew nothing at all.

THE DAY TORN

Frenzy, whether happy or not.
Reading, writing, cutting the lines out,
re-designed, erased, then penciled.

Often just closed up for the day
but immediately went back to my office,
re-did another line—another sign I'd made my point.

I had been *missing* myself,
but now all my poems
are my new life making a living.

Every page writing my lines,
slender as my pencil,
stiletto slitting a shape.

FLURRY OF SPEAKING

My own words were a flurry of speaking,
but it was me meaning nothing it all.

Words I knew were wildly different,
my language more than ever imagined.

Nothing now, never normally speaking
was the failing attempt by me to be me.

My *aphasia* started there,
        not yet learning to begin it.

HAVE A PIECE . . .

"I'll take a nap," I say,
but she said, "Have an apple."
What does she mean?
Give and take? Don't pay attention?

Oh, oh! Pissed me off.
She usually says, "Have a pear . . ."
Does she ever mean, "Have a piece?"
A different meaning?

I think, "Chicken, turkey, hamburger."
I would be better feeling safe
when looking at the moon at night.

Peace.

WHO KNEW?

Who knows what,
but who knew that?

The answer is not the question,
but who knew this?

I'm the only one

who has known

anything anyway,

not questioned when

what *did* this again.

And the question?
Well, the questioning

is done and anything
known, just not known, is.

ZIPPED ME UP

Did aphasia happen
to me/for me?

Somehow my brain-box
stopped and zipped me up,

zipped me up. A silent list
in a lift made and un-left me.
But didn't even touch my heart.

Stopped instead inside my hand.
Didn't even leave me
because it lost me first. Didn't hear Colleen.

Left and lost my own way.
Words talk and the end did break.

MY LAZY EYE

It wasn't a lazy eye
I had.

It was a curious eye,
sneaking a look to see

what the other one
was doing.

DARING, DARLING?

Darling, I used to love
meeting a new friend,
but learning again

to get a grip
right through my heart,
deeper than my breath.

What you and I knew
more daring you showed me,
but what flew my love away

suddenly missed me.
But darling, here we are.

Daring still.

SOMETIMES OR AGAIN?

Sometimes, whatever I'm doing,
I stop and try
to think about what I'm doing,

try to remember
what I had been doing
or wanted to do.

Lost my mind again
but learned to work
by reworking.

It's not bad working though,
even my additional time
this time.

YOU MOVE

We walk with us now knowing
what coronavirus to COVID-19 means.

Walking again each morning
we see emptiness

and walking with our dog
often no one else is near.

Who or what else is really
available now?

We are as lonely as the world is,
but even about the rest of us.

And what will the rest of us ever know?

OH, JUST TODAY

A poem I had written yesterday
truly touched me this morning,

even more than before.
Oh, God, I'd written my new words,
using the right dimensions.

I imagined singing or flying with the wind,
letting myself un-mangle again,
click-clack on with my business
to write what I have written lately.

How else could I feel losing myself?
It's as necessary as writing a poem.

DID I REMEMBER WHAT
KIND OF DATE IT WAS?

or what time,
or what occurred,

or who told you
about who also told me?

or is this ever
to be remembered?

or in the old days,
no time known knowledgeable

or does memory
re-memorize everything?

answer please—a list of words,
a book of poetry?

IF YOU KNEW

Long time I've been writing and re-writing poetry,
but loving how I now understand
the brilliant loss of my language.

Amazing, isn't it?
Saying what I'd *thought* I meant,
my little statements were not the right words.

How I work each day, crossing my fingers
that I got me here, I'm nervous a little and happy, but
I will never be the self I was.

IRIS

There's always an iris
amusing and amazing.
Today, wildly purple stretching
to search dark colors,
open and about to reach.
Reach.

Even the vase holds on,
shows courage for both
who touch the beautiful,
alive and color to color,
evoking how one can love another.
Longer to live, shorter to die.

MAKE A MASK AT THE BALL

"Make a mask" has switched.
Glorious focus, then again
a gleam and the glaze.

What would one say
about "wise eyes,"
or would it mean "see me"
or "fool me"?

Some flick or hiss,
but one says only, "who needs me forever?"

PALM SPRINGS

Watching a couple of girls
laughing loudly, splashing,
swimming to the edge.
It isn't only the pool.

What I know is you and me
watching all the women,
but really, we're standing closer,
feeling everything else.

I knew it was heat
swelling in me,
her arms around me,
sweet as she's warm.

This is everything later.
All in the bedroom.
Deeper than our bodies.
Swimming to it all.

TENSION

There's a viral world now, chaotic,
and our life's own ability
means wanting to survive and keep living.

The beautiful world
is still remembering us
and our passion isn't silent.

Loneliness comes and goes,
but our hope is strength
and continuing to promise us well.

We want remembering our strength
and hanging on, proudly hanging on.

MONDAY

When I wake up,
darkness is waiting.
It makes me nervous but
Colleen is still sleeping.

Flatten my comforter, cover my pillow,
take my iPhone, tap on doggie's bed.
Nikita is willing to go
and I lead her to the den.

First thing for me to do,
shut the house light off,
then shut my flashlight, too.
Orion is then what I see first.

Our early morning
is what I want to love.
Colleen comes slowly at first
and so I know—no chatting yet.

Every day
I intend to wait
and silently love her.
Again.

LESS THAN POSSIBLE

Your body parts don't always behave
but your fingertips feel like you've been on TV
and smooching my lips a million times.

What my hair cares about is you
amusing me and I want me
loving you perfectly.

Won't give up thinking we'll never end us.
Never.

WHAT DID I SAY?

I can't tell you if I can't hear
what you want me to say.
I can't remember
if I still knew what I meant.

Though intelligent enough,
I still struggle but practice
how to re-learn.
More forward, more backward.

An insane heart was mine,
engaging with simple words
and how I knew what to say.
I'm not so far away anymore.

IF YOU KNEW

Amazing, isn't it, when a brilliant loss of my language
was saying what I *thought* I meant
mine were not the right words.

I keep crossing my fingers,
happy and a little nervous
but I will be the self I was again.

Even now *feeling* differently,
I *lost* all my language.
No matter the date or length of life,
I have "me" back again.

IN THE DRYER

Today is sky-blue, but not as deep as lust.
Color emotion, too, and fingertips a "must."
Towels await the day and even more coming.

Music is fluffing T-shirts down and up,
hands folding as feelings do and pleasure later
top to bottom, everything the scent of clarity.

Oh, yes, and how do you wear your love again?

AT SOME POINT

I love working in my office
and I write or re-write almost every day.
Close my door and get to work,
make sure my fountain pen is ready to go.

Outside my window, spring colors
blooming again, water bubbling, too.

Even writing about what "phased" me,
my "aphasia" being available.

Every morning I say to myself,
"I've learned better"
and "me" never less than never,
truly knowing myself better now.

JUST IN CASE

I had to learn to remember
I had always loved you,
and something I've remembered about you
is now about me, too.

The one small line I kept missing
I thought my words were fine.
The language I was speaking was wrong,
but you gave me everything to save me, keep me.

I spoke sideways, hedged my meanings,
my brain no longer working.
Learning was what I worked with:
daily walking, smiling, laughing, trying.

My findable nouns and verbs
practiced language to get my "messages."
Walk every day, wake early.

Even what I missed before,
I love you still.

Remembering everything more.

SUSTAIN ME

My lips touching
the palm of your open hand
sustain me.

Cup your hand so close to my mouth
that you'll feel the wild river
whose bank you are.

I open again the palm of my hand
and you offer to keep me.
Never the end. Ever again.

BIOGRAPHICAL NOTE

Eloise Klein Healy, the author of nine books of poetry and three chapbooks, was named the first Poet Laureate of Los Angeles in 2012. She was the founding chair of the MFA in Creative Writing Program at Antioch University Los Angeles, where she is Distinguished Professor of Creative Writing Emerita. Healy directed the Women's Studies Program at California State University Northridge and taught in the Feminist Studio Workshop at The Woman's Building in Los Angeles. She is the founding editor of Arktoi Books, an imprint of Red Hen Press specializing in the work of lesbian authors. *A Wild Surmise: New & Selected Poems & Recordings* was published in 2013 and *Another Phase* in 2018.